CW00383212

A VIEW FROM THE
MIND'S EYE
AN ANTHOLOGY OF
MENSA POETS

Published by

HUNGRY OWL

LONDON
www.hungryowlbooks.com

ISBN 1-903808-07-3

Hungry Owl Books is a division of
Hungry Owl Publications Ltd.

PRINTED IN ENGLAND

What is MENSA?

Mensa is a worldwide organisation. It is a social club with the only joining qualification being that members have a high I.Q. The main aim of Mensa is to provide a stimulating intellectual and social environment for its members.

Mensa has absolutely no political or religious aims or associations whatsoever. Mensa is Latin for 'table'. It exists simply to provide a forum for intelligent people, who may wish to communicate, meet, and socialise with others of similar intelligence and intellectual capability. That is not to say that all discussion is about astrophysics (although that topic does crop up). There are many and varied hobby and interest groups within Mensa - one of which, for example, is a poetry club with its own magazine, gatherings and readings. Other activities range from serious debate and chess tournaments, to bungee jumping and fun fancy dress parties!

More information on MENSA is available at www.mensa.org.uk

So why MENSA Poets?

Curiosity, is the short answer. You don't have to be 'intelligent'
to write poetry, or do you? Surely the essence of poetry is to
convey feeling and emotion, rather than the cold facts and
formulas that 'high I.Q.'s' are expected to be good at. Is there,
somewhere within the psyche a link between intelligence,
and the ability to express emotion through poetry?

As with any group of people, Mensa encompasses a huge diversity of
individuals. There is only one common thread – all have a high I.Q.
Many Mensa members are expert computer programmers; strangely,
there are others who find a simple typewriter technically challenging!
And while a few members, despite their high I.Q. score, can hardly
string two sentences together, some others have a gift for encapsulating
observations and experiences into little cameo pearls – that are poems.

So, do Mensa members write good poetry?
Enjoy reading this book – and decide for yourself.

CONTENTS

CONTENTS

CONTENTS

GREG HOULGATE

MY DESK

This old oak desk knows full well,
The weary hours I have forced to keep,
As the swan quill toiled to weave its spell,
And a flickering lamp held back my sleep.

Long years my desk has lent support,
And borne silent the weight of a poet's trial.
It can just once, and once alone report,
These ancient labours were worthwhile.

When, tormented cruelly by a writer's rage,
A poem fierce I began to fashion.
My pen dashed the waiting virgin page,
'Til the paper blazed with passion.

The deed is done. The ink now dry.
At last! At last, I succeed!
But only this old oak desk and I,
Know the poem, no-one else will ever read.

MESSAGE IN A BOTTLE

A golden beach at sunset.
Surf wrestling grains of sand;
Polished by a billion waves,
At that place were sea meets land.

Stopping there to ponder,
'Will this go on for evermore?'
I spyed close by a bottle,
Being washed up on the shore.

Inside there was a message,
Scrolled tight within the glass.
What odd luck that now it finds,
Someone to read, at last.

Time stood still for an instant,
As the parchment slowly unfurled.
Revealing strangely written words,
As though from another world.

Excitedly I scanned the lines,
Eager to learn what it said.
Expecting a laugh, or at least to muse,
Until this message I read ...

To Whom may be Concerned,
From the Creatures of the Sea:

Beneath the waves we are dying,
You have us on our knees.
Cut down close by hook and net,
And ravaged with disease.
Poisoned by pollution,
Yet still you do not heed,
The ocean mothers as they cry,
For their little ones' lives they plead.

You have plundered and polluted,
All the Seven Seas.
We have given up everything,
Surrendered to your needs.
Beware the tide is turning,
What you reap is what you sow.
This message in a bottle,
Is our last and only hope.

What!? These things cannot be true,
Nor have much to do with me.
So I pushed the message back inside -
And threw it in the sea.

GET THEE BEHIND ME -
JANUARY SALES

Oh demon plastic, don't do this to me.
All year I have resisted a shopping spree.
Now January is with us and the urge grows strong,
To take plastic and cash and enter the throng.

The sales have started, I can't stay at home.
Anguished and biting sore knuckles to the bone.
To hell with recession, I've worked hard this last month.
To hell with temptation, I'll blow it all at once.

No expense spared in getting me there.
A black chariot, no less, a mere taxi fare.
Yes! There are the banners that make my heart bound –
'SALES' 'REDUCTIONS' '2 for £1'.

Elbows are everywhere as for bargains we fight.
I'll die for that jacket – it's love at first sight.
Whatever's behind that frantic scrum,
It must be worth buying, I want at least one.

Another shop, I can't pass up the chance,
For shoes such as these will make my feet dance.
It may take two hours to find the right pair,
But think of the saving, they'll last for a year.

No taxi fare left, I take the bus home.
Laden with bags, like a donkey I groan.
Tomorrow's reflections will be full of regrets.
The jacket's too loud,
          and the shoes they won't fit!

5. 6. 7. 8. WHO IS IT WE ALL HATE?

1 **ONE**
One is for the gun,
>   that went off in my hand.

2 **TWO**
Two is for the bullets,
>   I shot into a man.

3 **THREE**
Three is for the seconds,
>   it took to take his life.

4 **FOUR**
Four is for the women,
>   mother, sister, daughter, wife,

5 **FIVE**
Five is times a thousand,
>   the tears they must have cried.

6 **SIX**
Six is times a million,
>   or more that must have died.

7 **SEVEN**
Seven is for the Generals,
>   that start these bloody wars.

8 **EIGHT**
Eight is for the hate,
>   that goes on forever more.

9 **NINE**
Nine is for the drum,
>   that beats a marching sound.

10 **TEN**
Ten is when it ends,
>   then I can lay my damn gun down.

CAVATINA

How could you know, dear scribe,
what would touch my soul,
that melody you wrote for me,
all those years ago.

I hear you now through plaintive strains –
the pain you felt is mine.
The pain you must have known when
you penned your swansong, just for me,
all those years ago.

Never was it in vain, dear scribe,
the notes you wrote still haunt the ears;
hurt and heal so many hearts and minds.
Mine is but another to yield to your melancholy.

I hear you weeping in the strings
that sing sweet sad refrain.
Cavatina! Why me?
Why do you cut through my defences?

Is it the cello's slow note that torments;
or the quartet indulging in discordant harmony;
or the violin racked by such tremorous bow.

Yes, dear scribe,
I feel the pain in the notes you wrote,
just for me, all those years ago.

ONE BLOOD RED ROSE

Deep it grows to reach so low,
Drawing at the goodness there.
Threading down into the ground,
Caressing that which once was fair.

Standing proud above her grave,
Three years hence, its first full flower.
One Blood Red Rose declaring loud,
What lies beneath is now devoured.

Here Love lies silent, and alone.
Beyond my reach, tho' not desire.
This daring blight should be so bold,
To gloat its gain with petals afire.

How much I loathe that Blood Red Rose.
Roots stabbing down into the dark.
Deep it grows to reach so low,
Cutting through my love's still heart.

This blazon rose does mock me well.
Such, I must crush it in my hand.
Yet reaching out, a dew drop falls,
As tho' a tear into my palm it lands.

Perhaps I'm wrong to damn this bloom.
It has no thought, or less a care.
What is dead is gone, and Heaven knows,
All that remains - One Blood Red Rose.

JOY HARRIS

PETROL STATION FLOWERS
A CHRISTMAS PIG'S TALE
BILLY'S DREAM
CREATION
NOTE ON THE TABLE

PETROL STATION FLOWERS

Please don't buy me petrol station flowers,
If I'm not worth the extra, please don't tease.
Give me a glimpse of life, of inspiration,
Not a limp bunch of lame apologies.

Real flowers say 'happy birthday' or 'I love you',
These murmur: 'sorry, I was in a rush',
They've never seen the sparkling dew of morning,
Felt summer's warmth or cooling water's gush.

Poor things, it's not their fault, they have to nestle
Between the charcoal bags for endless hours,
Just to be grabbed by men who think they ought to
And thrown in stuffy cars, unfit for flowers.

So when I die, as they do – within minutes,
No flowers please, be generous in your giving,
To any garden club of your own choice
Which makes a life for plants that's worth the living.

A CHRISTMAS PIG'S TALE

Have you ever wondered why
A pig lives in a muddy sty,
While horses can recline in hay
And cows in greener pastures lay?

It happened that first Christmas Eve
When animals were forced to leave
Their open field and cattle stall
To visit the new Lord of all.

But one poor pig with cold and cough
Considered he should be let off,
He tried to tell, but had no choice,
The flu had made him lose his voice.

So angels came, as angels do,
And marched the creatures, two by two,
To pay their homage to the king,
The poor pig stood there, shivering.

He took his turn and tried to rout
The sneeze that tickled in his snout,
Alas for him that he could not
And showered the holy, swaddled tot.

There was a gasp from kings and clerics,
The Virgin flew into hysterics,
Then from shepherds came the cry:
"It's treason – and the pig must die."

They chased him out, o'er field and dell,
His life became a living hell,
They shook their crooks and yelled abuse,
The pig determined to break loose.

At last, as they bayed for his blood,
He found a pool of slimy mud,
And daubed his body, everywhere,
Till they ran past, quite unaware.

That might, an angel could be seen,
He spake: "They meat shall be unclean.
Thy tail shall short and curly be,
Thy life in mud, eternally."

The pig, resigned to fate, bowed low,
And since that Christmas, long ago,
Has lived the way the angel said,
With swill to eat, and clammy bed.

It would not be this way at all
If pigs had paracetamol,
So find yours now upon the shelf
And keep your sneezes to yourself.

BILLY'S DREAM

Billy shouted 'Big Issue' outside the Town Hall
Whatever the weather, till he'd sold them all,
He hadn't a home, a coat or a friend,
But he dreamed of a night out in London's West End.

To join the canals, he swam off down the Nene,
The boat people thought him the strangest sight seen,
They gave him hot soup and he backstroked away
To reach Oxford city before break of day.

The swollen Thames beckoned and carried him through,
Till the bright lights of London glowed into his view,
He found Leicester Square from the Westminster Pier,
But a top-hatted doorman yelled: "Get out of here."

He sneer at old Billy and turned him down flat,
He said: "You can't come in here looking like that;
There are fish in your pockets, there's weed in your hair,
Go down to the Arches – they have your sort there."

So Billy trudged off till he reached Waterloo,
There were kind, careworn faces, a few morsels too,
He told them his tale and they shared their stale bread
And declared: "You'll have Shakespeare tonight here instead."

Reg brandished a penknife and said "I'm Macbeth!"
Fat Arthur played Falstaff, with beer on his breath,
Mad Joe was King Lear ruling over the land
And Billy Prince Hamlet, cigar butt in hand.

They wrapped him with coats as he faded away,
The moon lit the Arches as bright as the day,
Billy smiled at old Meg, who played Romeo's wife
And said: "Thank you my friends, for the night of my life."

CREATION

Creation wasn't meant to be like this,
A frantic fumble in your old Capri,
At least the trolley man has left for home
And won't disturb us unexpectedly.

Did the earth move? Not in so many words,
The rusty heap just rocked from side to side,
It wasn't how I planned that it would be,
I watched, but never saw the stars collide.

I dreamt of moonlight and soft silken sheets,
Our faces lit by fragrant candle glow,
Not blinking in the orange streetlamp glare
With heavy metal on the stereo.

The god of lust shines down on us tonight,
It isn't love, if we should tell the truth,
Creation should be in all-powerful hands
Not those of over-sexed and mis-spent youth.

Beyond the tax disc twinkles one bright star,
Is that the child our union will create?
How will I tell him that he came about
One night when Sainsbury's closed at half past eight?

NOTE ON THE TABLE

So this is goodbye after 21 years,
It feels strange to be on my way,
We gave it our best shot – it wasn't enough
So better to call it a day.

There's nobody else, so no guilt is attached,
No recriminations or fuss,
When the children were gone we found nothing remained,
I wonder what happened to 'us'?

We pass in the night, so I'm reasonably sure
That my going will not break your heart,
Though we're no longer lovers, I hope that one day
We can learn to be good friends apart.

You'll find it quite different left here on your own,
When the shirt fairy's flown her last flight,
There'll be no one to nag when you're drunk with the lads
Or stare at the telly all night.

I'll find conversation with friends I've misplaced,
I'll laugh once again like before,
I've not just lost you but discovered myself
And found I quite liked what I saw:

A person with feelings, her own point of view,
An agenda and something to say,
Not somebody's mother or somebody's wife,
My life starts again from today.

PROFESSOR
ROBERT T. GREEN

VEINED LEAVES OF STONE
ICARUS THE MOTH
PROMETHEAN ICARUS
THE BOLTED DOOR
A RING WITHOUT AN AUDIENCE
FIRES OF ADVERSITY

VEINED LEAVES OF STONE

The year bells knell their promises
Of fossiled hopes.
The shadow list grows longer.

Tears are practised,
Easing hurts that overlap
To form a litany of ghosts
Who walk and talk
Along a mirrored corridor.
Dim voices, fading faces, passions spent,
Rattling the leaves of discontent.

ICARUS THE MOTH

Waxy wings
Sealed by the Sphinx
Whose silences spelt
Candled sunshine.

Bask in her radiance.
Fly into the flames,
Cradled by her six-armed comfort.
Plunge to where
Her strangled silences
Demand interpretation.

Far too late.

Foiled by misspent purposes,
Both hers and mine,
We neither of us
Dared discuss.

Largely because,
Knowing the answers,
Each preferred
To wait the day.

PROMETHEAN ICARUS

That I should love her fain so much
Speaks of a circumstance –
A circumstance where love,
Stunned out of reason,
Took refuge in a recklessness,
Borne orbital on wings of wax;
Spoke of a will
That essayed all the sun's intransigence
And lost.

Honed on her celebrations,
Centred on her muskiness,
My laughter died
As, falling through the heavens,
All my resolution cometed to cindered emptiness,
Wasting the desert of what might have been –
A might have been that never could have been
Without a miracle that never should have been
And never was.

We are but silly sparks with sentient pretensions
Flying from the flames of happenstance.
Blunted on the anvil of experience.
Waiting for the grace
Of sweet oblivion.

THE BOLTED DOOR

My wish to share
Was not her wish
Since I had nothing
She required.

Gifts were offered –
Graciously declined –
Or graciously accepted,
More silkily to ease my grief.

Eventually these tinsel gifts
Lost currency.
The key she held –
Invisible to her –
No longer worked the lock
She never knew existed.

Faced with a bolted door,
Hope curled.
Yet still I tried
To turn a key of glass
With sawdust fingers.

A RING WITHOUT AN AUDIENCE

She drowned.
My fault.

Her painted shade
Persisted in a parody
That spurned
My treachery,
Exacting tribute
Paid most willingly,
Not just
To glance the guilt.

Grim tumblers fell about
To turn the circus hurt
In both of us
And shelve the debt.

Unable to accept the loss
I fudged an issue
Neither of us
Wished to clarify.

Perfection nursed the seeds
Of putrefaction.

So now rank flesh
Must plug our nostrils,
Petrifying screams
Of silent protest.

I cannot understand her presence.
Which of us is meant to suffer?

She tortures both the clowns
For no good cause
That I can contemplate.

Dawn can herald
Only Nemesis
To close the cage.

FIRES OF ADVERSITY IN AN EVIL ARENA

Rosebud lips have thinned
To bitter disillusion.
Age has sent hope
Scuttling for refuge,
Cowed by evil.

Yet evil,
We are told,
Sets only the arena
In which the soul
Takes exercise.

Suffering   subsists
To shrive the soul
Provide the fire
In which base metal melts
And fighting steel
Be tempered.

The trouble is,
The exercise
May prove
Too energetic;

The suffering
May crack the soul
Before the self is lost
In otherness.

ERIC KARLSON

THE BISHOP'S TURNING BUDDHIST
IT'S A LOVELY DAY IN THE GRAVEYARD
FOR A DEAD CAT
THE GURU-GROUPIES
THE SEND-A-CHEQUE PROFESSOR

THE BISHOP'S TURNING BUDDHIST

The Bishop's turning Buddhist
And Mummy's just fourteen,
And Daddy's just a question mark
That no-one's ever seen.
Zoroaster's on the syllabus
With lots of other crap;
There's eighteen months in jail for Miss
If she gives a child a slap,
Criticise a wayward brat,
You'll cause a deathly hush,
Yet little girls use language
That would make a navvy blush.
Perverts have a licence now
To bugger teenage boys,
But give the boys a cigarette,
There's such indignant noise.
Manchester's a sexist word
And manhole's going too far,
And everyone's a graduate,
Stupidity's no bar.
Hindley's a social scientist
And mongols have the vote,
The Virgin Mary's great with child
By the Unholy Goat.

I vow to thee, my country,
We simply didn't know,
When we freaked out in the seventies
The way that things would go.

IT'S A LOVELY DAY IN THE GRAVEYARD

It's a lovely day in the graveyard,
And the ghosts are having fun,
Racing from the grassy turf
To the golden-splendoured Sun,
And doubling back to the earthly sphere
In an otherworldly spree
Riotously rollicking
In wild, ecstatic glee.
The ghosts of scrawny spinsters,
Rejuvenated now,
Fornicate among the graves
As only the young know how
And dusty elders of the Church,
From pleasures in life denied,
In spectral form belch drunkenly,
Pushing restraint aside.
And everyone's young and happy;
Great-Grandfather's a boy,
And God's in his manifestation
As Bacchus, Lord of Joy.
The Sisters of the Sacred Heart
Are skipping girlishly,
And Father Michael Murphy
Has a nun upon his knee
There's a party in the graveyard,
And they're laughing fit to weep,
At all the Earthly people
Who think they're fast asleep.
Oh, haste me to the party,
Oh, haste me to the feast;
Oh, haste me to the graveyard
When the trial of life has ceased!
It's a lovely day in the graveyard,
And the ghosts are having fun,
They know that when they're planted
Their lives have just begun.

FOR A DEAD CAT

Felicity Freekowtski Catkins Catchamouse, Siamese,
sleek and slim,
Undisputed mistress of her house, delicate, sweet and prim,
Commanded her servants to bring crunchies, and shrimps
of the very best,
Sweet Carnation, chicken, munchies, and a tin of red John West.
Willingly, gladly we all served her, watched her play and feast,
Grateful to know that we deserved her, queen of the mystic East.
Nine years old, and still a kitten, eyes of cobalt blue,
All who saw this girl were smitten; always she seemed new.
All too soon this goddess left us; not even a goodbye,
Age, and illness had bereft us; even a goddess can die.

Now she capers, leaps and rushes,
Catnip-sozzled, full of fun,
Where the fat mice grow on bushes
And the doggies cannot run,
There's a mystical dimension
Where the astral pussies play,
Look at dogs with condescension,
Tease the stupid mutts all day.
Caviar and cream are flowing;
Plenty fish for everyone,
And pussies worship the All-Knowing
Royal Lion of the Sun.
Cats are borrowers of the darkness,
Slinking smugly through the night,
Knowing full well, when they leave us,
They will walk into the Light.
Cats are needless of salvation;
Stay with us a little while,
Leave, and give no explanation;
Look at us from Heaven, and smile.

THE GURU-GROUPIES

(Affectionately dedicated to the memory of His Eminence the Very Venerable
Kalu Rinpoche, Incarnate Lama of the Karma-Kagyupa Lineage of Tibet)

We used tae be shorthand typists,
But tae Hell wi' all o' that;
Noo we live wi' these twa monks
In a wee monastic flat.

The flat's in a Buddhist centre
That's way oot in the hills;
A steady stream o' hippies
And a charity pays the bills.

The monks are incarnations
O' a weird Tibetan god;
And the wan wi' the baggy dewlap
Is a richt auld randy sod.

They say no' tae tell naeboady;
We've goat tae be discreet;
Officially we're hoosemaids
And we're laughin' fit tae greet!

We're the girls for the holy Lamas
Of Karma-Dharma-Ling,
And a' their rich disciples
Dinnae suspect a thing!

The wan wi' the baggy dewlap
Has a betting acoont wi' Hills.
And the wan wi' the stutter and the gammy leg
Is aye fu' o' booze and pills.

They say we're set fur Heaven
If oanly we dinnae tell,
And ony wee lassie whit grasses them up
Is sure tae gae tae Hell.

It's a far cry frae oor schooldays,
It's a far cry frae the Kirk;
But we're baith assured salvation -
And we dinnae need tae work!

THE SEND-A-CHEQUE PROFESSOR

I'm the send-a-cheque professor
With a shoddy pass degree;
I'm the answer to your problems;
Just send a cheque to me.

You've seen me in the tabloids
In two-centimetre ads
For muscle-building pamphlets
For desperate skinny lads.

I've got systems made for duffers
And methods that don't work,
All advertised convincingly
To every brainless berk.

A statistician's system
For winning on the nags;
A method by a gigolo
For picking up the slags.

How to make a living
In half an hour a day;
How to win the Lottery
Every time you play.

A compendium of systems
For winning on the pools;
An advert in 'Prediction'
Where I'm casting spells for fools.

My office is my bedroom
But the adverts say 'Suite B'
It makes it seem professional
And more on the level, you see.

I wrote my crap while on the dole
And now I make a mint;
I just sit at my computer
And do nothing but press 'Print'.

I'm the send-a-cheque professor,
And I'm laughing fit to bust
At your simple-minded innocence,
Inadequacy and trust.

I'm the send-a-cheque professor
With a shoddy pass degree,
And your greedy, grasping, gullible self
Is just fair game to me.

MARTIN REIJMAN

THE SUNBIRD STREAM
FUTURE ANGEL THEME
THE ISLAND OF GLASS
HIGHER THAN NOON

THE SUNBIRD STREAM

This time and place have made their space
Inside my weary mind.
The tranquil flow and sun filled glow
Have joyfully entwined.

Along the blue Sunbird, stand two
Old towers of light and truth:
Their elfin grace defends this place
Of beauty, peace and youth.

Long gone the men that lived here then;
Forgotten are their lores;
Long dead the lords who crossed these fords
And walked these crystal shores.

Slow beats this time-worn heart of mine
Beneath the azure sky.
The cool winds blow but all men know
That all who live must die.

And so l stay till end of day
Has tolled the evening bell.
And by the stream, a golden dream
Called God will ever dwell.

FUTURE ANGEL THEME

As wonderful as winterbirds and wheatfields in wild winds,
As timeless as a furtive glance from somewhere on the fringe,
Was love shared with that lady from my dream:
The perfect proof that things aren't what they seem.
The drops of scotch mist trembled in the mirror of the lake.
Her smiling, loving eyes lit up the days when I'd awake,
Her raven hair would flow out in the air.
She was a Venus, Medusa or was she nowhere?
Or was she you?

Below her soft and golden curls, her eyes were blue sapphires,
Revealing light from distant stars; her lips were like cool fire.
A girl like her could shake you to the core,
And push you to the edge, to cry for more.
We'd play guitars and sing of joy: our future angel theme;
I'd meet her in the choruses - her voice from crystal dreams.
She gave me famine and gave me a feast.
She was a fairy, a good wife, destroyer of peace.
Or was she you?

Then I was lured to wander off our road of unity,
On wayward paths and wasted time: frustrated lunacy,
Still haunted by the ghost of our goodbye,
And mazes of forgotten reasons why.
Now I've been looking for someone I thought was never born,
While burning leaves and autumn skies sing songs
                                        sad and forlorn;
But meaning has been struck down to the ground,
And torn emotions fallen and scattered around.
And so have I.
And so have I.

Now I have songs and lessons learned she's never known before.
Perception has enlightened me - I've opened all my doors.
But will she bleed forgiveness finally,
And will she let her love light fall on me?
Will she dance in turquoise mist when I call out her name?
Can we relive those days and will time wait for us in vain?
Could she be moonlight that shines in my soul,
To heal this cripple and make this dismembered man whole?
Could she be you?
Will you be her?
Just for a while,
Will you be her?

THE ISLAND OF GLASS

The moonlight was hazy, casting an eerie glow on everything around me.
I was waiting outside the ruins on top of the misty mound

I stared across the lake at Glastonbury Tor,
And stood in a silence that once buried me before
In the folds of a celtic king's cloak.
Nothing dared, and nothing stirred, none spoke.
Feral shadows in the trees and enchanted stones,
I was frightened of the strangeness deep in my bones.

I saw lights winding on a spiral path up the mountain on the holy island,
And heard fitfully on the night wind the sound of solemn chanting.
The soul knows   The soul knows

A sound like secret songs of soporific streams,
Reflecting wandering sprites in winter twilight dreams:
Unknown power that's not of this Earth,
Songs that fill the far-flung universe.
Through the swirling mist I saw a faint fleck of light,
Floating like a phantom, flickering through the night.

A familiar wind blew down to me from the ages long past,
From a battlefield of causes lost and the island of glass.
My heart was filled with forgotten grief and fear
                                        that I'd never known:
Of wild young eyes and impassive scars, and circles
                                of Standing Stones.

As the light slowly floated up the hill towards me,
I could see the figure of a man.
He was dressed in a black robe and hood, and then -
I saw his face...
The soul knows   *The soul knows*

His white beard, hawk-like face and deeply sunken eyes
That burned so hot and fierce that they could never die.
As he drifted past, I knew his name -
"Merlin - it's me - bring me back again!"
Then he peered into the dark, but saw nothing there.
And he frowned and turned to walk a path to nowhere...

HIGHER THAN NOON

Life's about to pounce but do you really care?
And it's something that your eyes will never see.
Minds have been scrambled but it's still crouching there,
And it's dying to expose your sacred sleaze.
Oh, the rich tycoon has danced on your cold bare toes again
And the hobo is loudly snoring in the sty.
And we all will sing along until everyone has gone
To the floral dance spring ballroom in the sky.

To the floral dance spring ballroom in the sky,
With a jaded winter's brass band on the stage.
Run off to the zoo and poke the lion's eye
And he won't linger longer in the cage.
Oh, the mercenary mates with the pacifist tonight
And my parents might be smooching in the hall.
We are floating on the moon; we are higher than high noon
In our glitzy fashion workshop in the mall.

In our glitzy fashion workshop in the mall,
With those lovely lacy curtains in your hair.
Sister does a tap-dance, climbing up the wall
While I look like a deranged Fred Astaire.
Oh, the manager has drooled on his brand new point-of-sale
And the shopper's fondly fondling all his wares.
But the smoker's in a haze and the crowd is in a daze
As the salesman tiptoes down the backstreet stairs.

As the salesman tiptoes down the backstreet stairs,
With his flashy ray-bans dangling from one ear;
Tommy guns are rattling while you brush your hair –
It seems that there is nothing left to fear.
Oh, the wind plays bottle songs and the drunk is staggering,
Still unconscious of a spreading yellow stain.
And he bounces off the wall, then he stumbles and he falls
In a foul untidy rag heap in the rain.

In a foul untidy rag heap in the rain.
And a lunatic mist settles down.
Blue moons keep on seeking mercy but in vain –
There is nothing left in this uncaring town.
Oh, four seasons have now passed far too quickly in your head
As your name is being summoned on the bleep.
You can heave a heavy sigh but you'd better wave goodbye –
Now the time has come to wake up from your sleep.

PAUL A. WILLIAMS

AN UNSOLVED CRIME
I DRINK THEREFORE WHO AM I
THE MAN IN GREY
TOO SOON

AN UNSOLVED CRIME

I wouldn't have normally sought your advice,
I don't even have any proof,
But while I was otherwise occupied ⁻ –
Someone made off with my youth.

I know it was here just yesterday,
It's come as a bit of a shock.
I haven't got everything out of it yet –
There were plenty of miles on the clock.

I just turned my back for a moment or two
To deal with more 'serious' topics.
I thought it was safe in the back of my mind –
How could I have been so myopic?

There were hundreds of uses I had for the thing,
And I hadn't got round to them all,
But now I suppose I'll just manage without ⁻
So my life has slowed down to a crawl.

I wanted it for its unceasing abundance
Of energy, zest and amazement
To help put the colour back into my world
That's growing as drab as the pavement.

I've searched all around in the junkyard of dreams
And I think I've discovered a clue –
Some half-buried memories of long-ago days –
'A la rechercher du temps perdu'.

It couldn't be much use without supervision,
I can't think who else would have wanted it, –
But somebody somewhere took off with my youth –
I suppose that I shouldn't have flaunted it.

I DRINK THEREFORE WHO AM I

I think I thought I said I knew
I wonder why I bother
I think I'll have to think again
of this, that and the other.

I wonder why I thought I'd said
I thought I thought I knew,
But after having second thinks
I haven't got a clue.

The only way to solve this is to
wear my thinking hat
In all my waking thoughts I never
thought I'd think of that!

A drink or two might help me through
this cogitative crisis
(Hmm. The only word that rhymes with that
is Gastroenteritis!)

To summarise my thoughts of late
might help my concentration
To think I nearly understood
The art of meditation.

But thinking about thinking never
solved a single clue
I drink another think might help
me work out what to do

So after all is dead and sun,
I drink therefore I'm drunk
I'll have to soon admit I can't
Remember wot I thunk.

I wonder why I wonder why
Another (hic) drink to you
I drink to think the bottle dry
... a rinky tinky doo ...

Of course, I know the answer now
It's easy when you're drunk.
I'm far too pissed to write it down
My brain has done a bunk!

THE MAN IN GREY

(Inspired by a story about a millionaire who willed his entire fortune to a complete nonentity simply because 'He's never interfered with my life in any way, shape or form that I'm aware of')

Let's drink a toast to Algernon Bartholomew Du Pré -
Who's never buggered up my life (or yours) in any way,
(Of course you've never heard of him; he's called the 'man in grey') -
He's basically a cipher, and prefers his life that way.

Let's drink a toast to Algernon Bartholomew today -
He spends his time arranging his chrysanthemum display,
And making animated films with little blobs of clay,
Essentially a waste of space, and that's the way he'll stay.

Let's drink a toast to Algernon, in my book he's okay -
No good at conversation - he's got nothing much to say.
He never makes advances as he's neither straight nor gay;
When Algernon was born, God must have looked the other way.

Let's give three cheers for ABDP, hip hip and hooray,
He's never crossed my path to screw me up in any way,
He's difficult to pick out in a crowd of one, they say -
He's free from all ambition, independently passé.

Let's drink to Algy, there's a chap who knows his place to stay;
His mother used to drive him mental every single day -
He would have been a politician if she'd got her way,
Thank God he stayed anonymous, that's all I've got to say.

So raise your glass to Al and his assorted shades of grey,
He'll never cut you up in traffic in his Chevrolet,
Or overtake your car to pinch the only parking bay,
Or turn up on your doorstep trying to sell you toilet spray,
Or try to 'Organize your life the new Organic way',
Or jump the queue you're waiting in to grab the last soufflé,
Or help you pack your shopping bags and drop the Beaujolais,
Or mix you up with someone else and spoil your holiday,
Or bore you at a party with his exploits in Bombay,
Or leave your bath tap on and saturate your underlay,
Or get blind drunk one night and throw up in your alleyway,
Or wake you up by practicing his E-flat cor anglais,
Or turn up on your wedding night and steal your fiancée,

No, Algy's talent is unique - I hope he'll always stay
Completely absent from my life - I like him best that way.

TOO SOON

Tell me you love me, she said
a week since first we kissed.
A smile was all she received –
her request was hard to resist.

Tell me you love me, she asked
the next encounter we shared.
I fumbled a kiss, then departed –
my emotions had to be spared.

Please say you love me, she whispered,
I need to hear your voice.
I battled the urge to respond,
not wanting to make the choice.

Just say it once, she pleaded –
I had to release the pain.
I tore the words free from my heart...

I never saw her again.

JUDITH THOMAS

WHEN I WAS TEN
WAR LORDS
THE NEST BOX
DEAD NEWS

WHEN I WAS TEN

That bath from base to brim
Voluminous water flowing;
He'd turned the tap, (t'was always **him**),
Ecology unknowing.
For us, in stupor to assess
The time he took to make this mess.

Down on the railway, 'A' to 'C'
Two trains in competition.
One slow, one fast, to pass at 'B'
Eternal repetition.
We tussled with this time-table
To fix 'B"s point in steamy fable.

Now all those marbles - sixty-four
For sale at differing prices;
Say tuppence small, but nine were more
To cause a mental crisis.
We had to know, and should have cared,
The loss or profit thus declared.
Now long divide a given figure,
Five thousand and seventy two,
By thirteen or so, but nothing bigger,
One answer's a hundred and two.
These problems, with their cohort 'n'
Beset my time when l was ten.

WAR LORDS

They seek in vain for one to play their part
to conquer force; make power a mode for life.
So each with each from harmony will start
to banish war, to cause the end of strife.
Vain nations with the bomb remain aloof,
their atom smashers clearly giving proof
to mounting capital. So how should those
with other gifts compete? How hold, compose,
restrain from terror as the shots are hurled
to maim, deface, disable? Hide from foes;
for no-one's god advances all the world.

All politicians blunder in a haze
to tell the defects secret in each land.
Explain, decide, then into wreckage raze
constructed wealth: each other countermand,
all precedence tangental. Submission
luring brickbats; non-violent derision?
There is no way to tread a path of peace;
we lurk in caves, in bunkers flags unfurled;
invoking gods whose mass might bring release,
for no one god advances all the world!

Call Buddha, Christus, Jaweh, Shekinah
in judgement. Let all try poor, aspiring
man, whose chaos topples right. Phenomena
whose motives rest on Id: the king
of all the earth must seek defeat. Sacred
beings split; dismantled nuclei, death-heads
opposing truce leave broken bodies torn
by gods. They should debunk, regroup, return to
Dis. Their skills deploy to rule the underworld.
Then, freed from idols, man might begin to learn
that no one god advances all the world.

THE NEST BOX

"Come here my sweet and look at this
It's been here all the winter;
Hard by that fruit which tastes of bliss,
It needs some looking inter".

His gyrate head he shoved inside
While she stood on the roof
"You should agree to be my bride
And not remain aloof."

She nibbled nuts while giving thought
To his arrogant proposal.
Should she object to being caught?
Commitment seemed colossal.

He woos her with melodious tune
(Asserting he is boss!)
He hops inside, she's in a swoon,
He's found their thalamos.

DEAD NEWS

Assassins—heed the call to kill the news,
make sacrificial act. Go thrust long knives
full through, destroy all heart. No pall survives,
nor meddling democratic pretence to excuse
the spattered media corpses. Denuded screens
stare blankly into space. Strange worlds glare back
from absent voids, unsure of what they lack.
Spinning free, possessed by giddy indigenes,
before its death the news unseen, unheard,
formed apathy of gore. Consumers turned, then moaned.
Rare poets, politicians, pious priests were stirred.

TOBY WREN

THE OWL
FOREVER AUTUMN
GHOSTS (double acrostic)
ALMOST SO
MENSA TEST

THE OWL

The owl, though blessed with perfect sight,
will sleep all day and fly at night.

These circumstances, though exact,
result in a peculiar fact

that male and female rarely meet
and are considered most discreet.

And what then is an owl to do,
that sadly lacks the wit to woo?

FOREVER AUTUMN

How gently now the seasons turn and fall:
the ebbing tide of each sequestered year.
The pageant well rehearsed from cuckoo call
to autumn gold... and winter silver near.

The wet and weary woods; these days we share
where drifting mists sift through the silent trees
and whispered secrets haunt the chilling air.
How softly now, these memories that tease

an idle moment into words and rhyme.
The mystery of love that must evoke
a sonnet spoken of this gentle time
we share, beneath the broad and bronzing oak.

And far beyond the grey of wintry skies
forever autumn lingers in your eyes.

GHOSTS (double acrostic)

Ghosts are waking - phantoms floating,
haunting ruins... drifting through.
Omens dark with warnings too!
Spectral souls and apparitions -
troubled wraiths of grim debut
stirred to each grave rendezvous.

ALMOST SO

Your time of leaving is not now
though you have gone, or almost so.
Gone from the bright days that endow
a sense of loss, so when you go
it will serve to confirm, somehow,
a truth that we already know.

We meet, as friends departed meet:
a casual smile... a brief hello.
The chanced encounter on a street
with little left to say, although
such thoughts as dwell remain discreet -
for you have gone... or almost so.

And will I know and will I care
when you have gone? How may I know
what thoughts remain, or be aware
of what you take the day you go?
A measure of the thoughts we share
and memories that will not show
yet wait, like ghosts, already there -
for you have gone ... or almost so.

MENSA TEST

The quadrangle has witnessed better days.
Grey paving slabs tilt, choked by weeds between
their mossy gaps - defiant of man's hand.
A wall of crumbled, yielding brick displays
the journal of past seasons – seems to lean
as if the school had such frail beauty planned.

A sudden swirl of brown and brittle leaves
lifts briefly in the breeze - the tang of salt
from coastal waters sharp upon the air.
A sagging iron gutter, weeping, grieves
that summer afternoon will fail to halt
the flake of paint... the rust of iron laid bare.

And here I sit : with pen and paper wait
for Nancy, while the sun glares overhead -
as if aware where slanting shadows hide
the ghosts of yesterday. This turn of fate,
that sees her footsteps back through childhood led
to classroom test. She studiously inside

to brink the limit of her mental skill,
and work through logic thought - cerebral play
of word and number, spatial art and shape...
The swing of dappled sunlight in the still
and hushed late afternoon erodes the day,
to bring a timed conclusion and escape.

Then homeward with excitement and relief!
Comparison of tests – mine faded now,
hers bright as laughter... certain as her smile
of cautioned confidence. Assured belief
of time well spent and likewise mine, somehow.
Words folding into patterns all the while.

RUTH TWYMAN

MIRACLE OF THE TREES
THE OVERLOAD
PHANTASMAGORIA
THE WATER GARDEN
THE OPEN GRAVE (OF A HEDGEHOG)

MIRACLE OF THE TREES

Sear skeletons of trees, their cold limbs shaking,
Blackened and gnarled against the winter sky.
The dead that won't lie down. Their undertaking
To see Eternity before they die

Hold cold the wind. It will not give an answer.
Its tongue licks carelessly around each frame,
As sensually vapid as a dancer,
It sidles closer, whispering a name.
The name is horrible, and begs no hearing,
And all the branches shiver at its sound.
The shriek of sap climbs high within the tree trunk.
A tremor echoes through the frozen ground.

The wind is gone and sunshine bathes the treetops.
A benediction for the year ahead.
Upon the bones, new green flesh is appearing
And Lazarus is risen from the dead.

THE OVERLOAD

Quietly it creeps in, the crush,
Insinuating over years.
Caught in skeins of silver blush,
It manifests our inmost fears.

And slowly, as the liquid rises,
 With no overflow to check,
We soak up spills of life's surprises;
Take it neatly in the neck.

Drip, drip, drip, as our strength falters,
Though we try and try and try,
Our perspective of life alters,
And we slowly start to die.

No one sees our inner ending,
For the shallow smiles remain,
And our dutiful unbending
Masks a plethora of pain.

Till, at last, there is no farther
That, as humans, we can go.
Living has become much harder
Than we ever thought we'd know.

Time to break the onward journey;
Time to leave the carousel;
Time to be our own attorney;
Time to win time off from Hell.

This is not the end of being.
This is not the terminus.
This is just the point of seeing
That this is the time for us.

PHANTASMAGORIA

Phantasmagoria.
Tell us a story we'll never forget.
Titania and Oberon.
Turn the dream over on suns as they set.

Watch the dream. See it glide
Over the open tide, into the sea.
Tunnel the bubbles round.
Funnel the double sound down to the tree.

It blanches above the waves,
Branches, like churches' staves, into the sky,
Finding the sun again,
Blinding the sight of men; eye for an eye.

Into the sounding realm,
Bounding the empty helm, echoes arrive;
Each a facsimile.
Each one backs in on me. Bees to the hive.

Buzz of a million wings.
Us, and a trillion things waiting to find.
Time to elapse, and new
Neurons, synapses through slumbering mind.

Magical lantern show.
Show us the phantom go out to the crowd.
Shadowy though it seems,
Outlining all our dreams behind your shroud.

You have the dream we share.
Float on the keening air, each breath we take.
Carry our hearts away
Until now starts the day, and we awake.

THE WATER GARDEN

Where, in a million dreams, could we foretell
A garden teeming with such loveliness?
Wrought from the sea; its bosom and its swell
And wind sown with a motherly caress,
The garden grows.

A plethora of function, and of form;
Each organism carries in its heart
The water molecule whence it was born.
And, as its myriad cells divide and part,
The garden grows.

Unseen by us, our very lifeblood flows
Within its intricate and verdant veins.
To spite our face, we will cut off our nose
Until, as nothing of our world remains,
The garden dies.

THE OPEN GRAVE (OF A HEDGEHOG)

Under the railway bridge he lay,
Jaws agape; skin shrinking from the bone;
His vital force extinguished, like a flame,
To close and die, as we all die, alone.
I couldn't look. It didn't seem quite right
To gaze into an open grave.

And then the winter came.
Dust unto dust. Snow unto snow.
And Nature threw her whitened ashes in,
Whispering a prayer.
And, when the snow had gone,
He wasn't there.

WALDO

A TALE OF A FACE
THE ROAD
REPEAT PERFORMANCE
ONLY THE DISTANT PAST

TALE OF A FACE

This is the tale (not the tail) of a
face. (It can't be the tail, that is in the
wrong place). First take the cranium as it
is called, stubbly or hairy (unless it be bald).
Strongly protecting the great human brain, that
gives us control of this earthly domain. But
don't let that fool you, this part of my verse,
isn't the cleverest, though not the worst. **As**
we go on you'll be bored by it all - I **almost**
forgot and left out the eyeball. Well, **never**
mind, now I've come to the nose. (This
would be much simpler written in prose).
Shaped in all styles such as Roman and Greek,
Negroid, Semitic, short, long, strong and weak.
Pretty and ugly and covered in hair, I could go
on but I think I'll stop there. After the nose
comes the stiff upper lip, (that's if
you're English - the rest are quite
limp). After the lips com**es the old**
North and South, commonly known
to us all as the mouth. Then, just
below, is the jaw (or the chin),
sometimes found under
a fatuous grin. Then just
the neck remains, right
at the base, but I don't
think I'll bother, it isn't the face!

THE ROAD

The rain falls, and the shining curve
Of Macadam will glisten for
An hour or two and then, sun dried,
Continue with its static pride
Towards the sea, and skirt the shore,
Then turn full circle, counties wide.

Here, bedded soft between green fields
A breathing space and little toil,
Then a cool place beside a weir.
The country air is fresh and clear,
With no harsh city fumes to spoil
The sweet scent of a farmer's fire.

Then a long bend and the fields end,
The road clutters and grows gutters.
A paved sidewalk, the sound of talk,
And the rows of houses beanstalk.
A town's near and the road mutters,
And girds its loins with threads of chalk.

And its inner metal tenses
For the traffic that is coming,
The inevitable clamour
Of a town's metallic stammer.
Cables strumming, engines humming,
And the crash of a steam hammer.

Fighting past the intersections
Where the baleful eyes blink redly,
And the traffic madly scuffles
Back and forth in endless shuffles,
Like some manic maestro's medley
Played through steel and concrete muffles.

Through the city's teeming centre,
Thoughts of brook and pond and runnel,
Bridging a polluted river,
Thoughts of trees that do not wither,
Creeping through a concrete tunnel,
Mind with country thoughts aquiver.

Now the city's roar is fading
And the trappings of its kingdom
Are behind, and the country calls.
"Come road, come welcome to my walls
Of hedge, and to my fields of freedom".
And the road smiles, as the rain falls.

REPEAT PERFORMANCE

What, soldiers marching? My old eyes
Are getting worse. What's that you say?
The sound of feet a-tramping? No,
I can't hear much at all today.

I thought it was the cattle, bound
For market. Usually they are
On Tuesday afternoon you know,
What's that you say? Another war?

I haven't read the papers much
These past few months, my eyes are bad.
And so you see, I didn't know
They'd started fighting, that's so sad.

Not sad you say? Well, maybe so.
The glory's there all right for some,
And marching columns make a show
For those with eyes to see them come.

The flags and banners waving free,
The trumpets and the marching drums,
The honours and the battle scars
Are fine, for those who have no sons.

What? No, I have no child young man.
But once I had an only one.
I have his picture here, and look,
These are the medals that he won.

...Oh dear, he's gone. They never stay,
To listen to my foolish tongue,
Old medals and dead pictures mean
So very little to the young.

ONLY THE DISTANT PAST

The years flow faster now than long ago,
Events pass transiently.
Outdistancing my memory,
And disappearing like a shadow show.

Quick flowing through the changing scenery,
The images speed by my failing eyes,
Too close, to quick for me to recognise.
The past alone moves slow enough for me.

For when I dream that old reality,
I live again as in those long gone years.
My sight is clear in spite of ancient tears.
Only the distant past is close enough to see.

ELIZABETH SPENCER

MOTORWAY MADNESS
LOCKED IN A WORLD OF THEIR OWN
TRAVEL FEVER
SUPREMACY

MOTORWAY MADNESS

Six o'clock in the morning
And the weary drivers,
Blinking away the fog of sleep,
Pour relentlessly - bumper upon bumper,
Lights blinding, flashing, horns sounding
Lane changing - to work.

The throbbing of the radios' cacophony
Faces them, as blinded by their thoughts
They drive seeing yet unseeing,
Their only care - their own ultimate destination.

A yellow, sulphuric pall shrouding the motorway
Goes unnoticed until in a moment of panic
The lorry driver slams on his brakes,
Jack-knifes.

And catapulting vehicles zigzag
Driving too fast, too close,
Careering hither and thither
With wild abandon.

The air is filled with the screaming
Of metal wrenched;
Of bodies broken, burnt, maimed,
Dead.

Motorway madness once more
Has collected its toll.

LOCKED IN A WORLD OF THEIR OWN

Staring vacantly into space,
The mumbo - jumbo of the outside world
Is locked out.
Instead, a brilliant existence floats.
Turns into psychedelic patterns.
Tumbles, twists, turns,
Leaps and dances over rainbows.

The eyes, impervious of all around,
Are locked,
Hypnotised by their own
Unique visions. dreams,
Travelling on and on
In never - ending nothingness,
Entranced.

Hour after hour,
Day after day,
Year after year,
The catatonic state engulfs
In never ending perpetuity,
Obedient to a call,
Unhearing to the voice,
Resting in their shell. Silently,
without objection
In whatsoever pose
Wheresoever, for as long
As others demand. Subservient.

They have given up the hurly burly of life.
Given in to the demon pace
That every day demanded
And have found tranquillity,
A nearness with their creator.

We long for them to share our hectic activity
Our never ending turmoil
We are saddened by their state we cannot understand,
Yet should we not delight for them?
Give thanks that they have found
A living peace
Reserved usually for death?

TRAVEL FEVER

The headlights beam down at me
From the heavens.
Port and starboard, red and green wink.
Beckoning me skywards.
I have travel fever again.
I'm a jet-setter, go-getter
I fly
Out of fast and furious airports
Where whining children mingle
With their cavorting peers.
Weary travellers lay outstretched
On plastic benches
And others stumble over rucksacks
Or hand luggage defying description.

A ballet of aeroplanes
Weave and bob gracefully in the sky
Urging me upwards.
My passport, dog-eared bursting
With rubber stamps and visas
Takes me by the hand
And guides me yet again
Through passport control
Where familiar faces nod in greeting.
It leads me onto the giant bird
Which will transport me onwards
Until I reach that foreign clime.

So back and forth I fly
Home to home, office to office,
Never wearying of being, for some brief hours,
One of the stars.

SUPREMACY

Stone tentacles point up aloft with claws of pristine white.
Majestic power over men who tremble at its sight.
Those, ice-pick claws deface the skies; that monumental girth
Dismisses mortals in its wake; its roots beneath the earth.

Like wedding cake, tier upon tier, the mountain towers tall
Resplendent in its awesome power, a white and wondrous wall,
Defiantly it stands erect, omnipotent, supreme.
Yet conquering its snow-bound peak is many a climbers' dream.

Few have survived to tell the tale, and many have succumbed
Their bodies hidden in the snow; their loved-ones ever numbed.
What influence does this edifice exert upon mankind
To make them climb the highest mount, leave sanity behind?

With nerves of steel and courage blind, with expertise and prayer,
They take the highest route on earth to shelter 'neath God's lair.
On mighty crags where nothing grows, they stoically take the test
To prove human supremacy out splendours Everest.

LILJAY

NORTHERN SPRING
FLOWERS FOREVER
I COME TO GAUGE THE TEMPER
OF THE FIELDS
KITCHEN LADIES
MRS MILLMAN

NORTHERN SPRING

This time last year
Trapped in Spain
Longing for the daffodils
Longing for the rain
I looked upon my palm trees
Trying to rejoice.
Penned them all a song of praise
In a foreign voice –
But now I have the Real Item
Spread before my eyes,
The buds, the birds, the crocuses,
The truly British prize:
The fields so green, an emerald
Has nothing to compare,
The soggy garden promising
A tulip, red and rare.
The wind is like a kitchen knife.
My car is caked in mud.
But I'm energised and singing,
Being Northern in the blood!

FLOWERS FOREVER

Flowers forever fading
As I try to find the pattern,
Ever closed, ever closed
As I linger in the daisies

Flowers forever turning
On a ground of midnight blue
As I skip among the colours
And I finish up with you

And you hold me and you turn me
As we melt into the pattern
Ever turning
Ever turning

And the colours ....
Disappear from view.

I COME TO GAUGE THE TEMPER OF THE FIELDS

"I noticed you turned left"
My neighbour said the other day
"But right would be a shorter direct way
To work"
I smiled,
Did not tell him that
I come to gauge the temper of the morning fields
To see the way the windswept hawthorn yields
To the elements, and how the beech
Glints in the ascending sun
Ranked lamps at Locking Stumps sing to me in unison
A choral ditty deep in concrete note.
Leaping the tangled motorway I gloat,
Breathing farmyards and the first frosts,
Counting magpies in third gear,
And aiming through the hole in Winwick spire
My morning prayer.

KITCHEN LADIES

Kitchen ladies are you bored?
Take a chance and go abroad.
See the way you wield your trolley,
Splosh the soup
Or Plonk the Jelly.
"Tis the same the whole world over
From Tenerife to the Straits of Dover.

Cleaning ladies, you could have
The nasty puddles in the lav
Translated into Deutsch or Frog,
And learn the foreign word for Bog.

Kitchen ladies, learn to say
In a new and different way,
'Macaroni on the floor'
'Pass your plate' and 'Who wants more?'

Cleaning ladies with a mop,
Practise in another tongue,
How to say 'Get out!' and 'Stop!'
Before you die of smoker's lung.

MRS MILLMAN

Mrs. Milllman cannot take
The Summer heat
She stands perspiring in her shop
While candybars grin, greaseproofed
At her hot distress.
And chocolate runs.
The store's a mess.
Ken's gone to watch Bill Coleman win the bowling match again
And Trade is slack ......
The only sounds
Are Lynne and Tracey
Round the back,
Skipping holes in melted tarmac,
Evidence. like fingerprints on cake
Of stolen joy which stolen time can make.
They're meant to be at school. not Uncle Ken's.
Mrs. Millman sighs and wipes her specs
And leaves a misty mark upon the lens.
She'd like to jump into the fridge ......
But even that is fighting
And complaining in the heat,
And on the top –
A bluebottle has found a sticky sweet.

MORWENN EVANS

THE COPPERPLATE LADY
CASTLES IN THE AIR
A GIRL CALLED LONELY
LONDON UNDERGROUND

THE COPPERPLATE LADY

The pages, old and stiff,
Brittle now from neglect,
Turn reluctantly. Here and
There is a note written in the
Margin – a comment by a word
In neat copperplate hand.
Her name and the date are
Marked in the front – she'll be dead
By now without a doubt,
The copperplate lady.
Then a crease of paper whispers
To the tiles and I open
A letter to the young copperplate lady
From someone close and loving;
And the lady steals like a butterfly
Into the room and as I
Breathe her scent and hold
Her icy cold hand, I know that she
Is still alive,
However dead she may be.

CASTLES IN THE AIR

Darling, Mummy says she doesn't mind,
Though Daddy doesn't know.
It's better not to tell him –
He wouldn't let me go.

I'm awfully excited –
At last I can be free!
Us two in the big, big world
Alone, just you and me.

Mummy asked me if I loved you.
"Mummy, dear, of course I do!"
She didn't understand, though,
My total devotion to you.

When can we be married?
Oh! Soon I hope it is.
I've loved you for two weeks now,
Ever since our first shy kiss.

A GIRL CALLED LONELY

Listening to next-doors conversation.
One pair of shoes by the door.
Not laughing out loud at TV shows.
Eating from the pan.
Looking forward to going to work.
Yawning with boredom, not exhaustion.

LONDON UNDERGROUND (9.3.88)

On the Tube one Saturday night,
Drunk and hysterical as usual,
I sobbed.
The old man opposite
Looked into the darkness
Looking for light.
He sniffed at my unhappiness,
And shuffled.
He smelled of week-old vomit,
And I wrapped my cleanliness
Closer round me,
Crying into my hanky.

My tears subsided
As I watched the tramp's eyes,
White like a statue,
Looking,
Dead with looking.

"Does this train go to Heaven?"
He never even moved his head
To ask me that,

"I keep getting on trains,
Looking for Heaven,
And none of them go there."

All the other passengers were silent,
Staring at the old man
Who had dared to say
What *he* was looking for
In the darkness.

I smiled.

"Now, that's a little piece of Heaven,
A woman's smile."
Warm blue now, his eyes twinkled.

I walked home calm.
It was a clear cold night.
I looked up at the dark sky.
I looked at the closed shops,
Closed pubs, closed doors
And dark windows.
Nothing to look at.
So much to look for.

MOHAMMED MIAH

PERIHELION
PHOENIX
ETHICS
PARTING
SEASONS

PERIHELION

We sat at the edge with our feet in the water.
My hand flowing through the stream
Flowing through the air,
Through long red hair.

Quiet and wonderful.

Then ... I grew sad,
For I knew
That it
would
End.

PHOENIX

Beyond the massive mountains,
Upon the valley floor,
Dense lies the thickset forest –
Wherein the cloistered soul.

A thousand years of living
(a thousand years within).

A barren bough to perch on
Amongst the leafy mass.
He thrives on isolation
Where tension holds him fast.

And suddenly.

The wolf is loosened
It bounds from a fissured eye.
Tearing through the thickset forest,
Over the valley floor.
Sweeping across the massive mountains –
It comes
To kill us all.

ETHICS

For a life of equal measure
You must learn to divide
And be equidistant
To all sides.

When in endless search
Of the golden mean,
Ever try to balance
All that has been

And seek life at the fulcrum
Of earthly extremes –
Living days without passion
And nights without dream.

PARTING

Across the breach that staggers
There goes a careworn sigh.
It rises for a moment
Then falls down to die.

A remembrance of the instant
That raged within a cry.
It had risen for a moment,
Then fell down to die.

A wish that could not ever,
Until you said goodbye.
It lingered for a moment,
Before it fell – and died.

SEASONS

Gentle flows the summer
But Autumn has the key,
For in that thoughtful season -
First you came to me.

Icy falls the winter
But Spring brings greater pain,
For in that thoughtless season -
Last you called my name.

Season unto season,
Now, all seem one to me,
For what was once is not
And never more shall be.

JEAN HAYES

DISCOVERIES
TERRITORIAL
MISCHANCE
SANTA GOES TO CHURCH

DISCOVERIES

I sometimes think, before we're in our coffins,
Every last secret will be probed
By scientific boffins.
Have they at last a route map of Creation?
Do masses of neutrinos fill the void
Between the stars? Will humans land on Mars
Or face annihilation by an asteroid?

Each day we peep inside Pandora's box
Forcing the lid a fraction - spray the flies –
We pop a pill or tweak our body clocks;
Pretend we're wise.

The information I am puzzling over
Is down to earth and boring (please don't yawn).
I wish, before I die, I could discover
Who owns the dog that messes on my lawn.

TERRITORIAL

Primitive urges start to flow
When we are short of space.
A neighbour watches.
When you go his car is in your space.

You try hard not to fret and swear,
You turn the other cheek.
No good. Next time you move, he's there.
You stand it for a week.

At last you hammer on his door.
He grins, and then you know
You'll hit him one day. This is war
And friend has turned to foe.

MISCHANCE

Twice have I loved immodestly, though for the briefest span.
Inspired by youth's naivety I found the Perfect Man.
On London's teeming Underground, approaching Leicester Square
We pledged our souls in bliss profound across the moving stair.
Wild ecstasy soon wore a frown; starving, I could not sup
For he, alas, was going down and I was coming up.

In middle age I scorned all men. Passion was deemed absurd
So I was inattentive when the second strike occurred.
One rush-hour night at Turnpike Lane, assuming no disguise,
My second love with message plain transfixed me with his eyes.
How full of bitterness the cup that toasts a broken clown,
For this time—he was going up,. And I was coming down.

SANTA GOES TO CHURCH

About a hundred years ago, when Christmas cards were new
And nothing much was in the shops,
                              young Santa's moans were few.
Most children's Christmas present was an orange in a sock,
So down those chimneys he would slip,
                              no need to watch the clock.
He'd done by daybreak, job complete, but people wanted more.
They built huge smoky factories making toys and games galore.
One day, in desperation, Santa went to church and prayed:
"I'm in the wrong career," he groaned.
                              "Mistakes are being made."
Now when the Lord heard this he said
                              "It's not your fault old chap
Hard lessons must be learnt. Be patient. 1 will set a trap".

So Santa smiled, but not for long, since some

one thought of clones

And Santas popped up everywhere, complete

with mobile 'phones.

They suffered all the ills of men: depression, disc collapse,

Loud ringing in the ears - and then some

people thought, perhaps

An element of greed was creeping in. We've too much stuff

While half the world is starving. Time to say enough's enough.

Let's start to live more simply. Spread the word. Create a force

For Good, to save the Planet (it was God's idea, of course).

There'll be some unemployment. Santas, you can leave the race

In round about ten years. It's called downshifting.

Watch this space.

JOHN EXELL

JOB SEEKERS' PSYCHOSIS
MY ELECTRONIC LOVER
POETIC MOON BEAM
THE FIVE SENSES

JOB SEEKERS' PSYCHOSIS

(Written during the recession)

I seem to have contracted Job Seekers' Psychosis.
I first noticed it the other day.
Job adverts began to swim before my eyes.
I could read other things, all except job adverts.
I went straight home and went to bed,
Saying to myself, "It's another day tomorrow."
But when tomorrow came, I couldn't get up.

When I finally did, and went out,
My legs refused to move
in the direction of the job centre.
I told them to, but they wouldn't,
They went the other way.
Even in the library,
My hands refused to open
the newspapers at the job section;
Instead my eyes would only read the funnies,
And a piece about someone
Caught with a parliamentary whip in their hands.
I'd stopped reading my stars long ago.
They always said something like,
"Play your cards right
and promotion is on its way,"
Or "Love blossoms in the workplace today."

I went to the doctor.
I told him that I had Job Seekers' Psychosis.
He looked at me blankly,
Then he took a large book from the shelf, thumbed through,
And declared,
"It's not here. It's unknown to science."
How did I feel? What were its symptoms?
I said they were extreme anger.
A strong desire to see a change in government.
Even go to Westminster
armed with a machine gun.
A desire to join the Workers Revolutionary Party.
Wanting to publicly throttle
the next person to say,
"Haven't you got a job yet?"
Or "Get a job!
There's plenty of work if you look for it,"
And other such comments
A desire to hand grenade
the people working at the job centre,
With all their smarmy looks.
If it wasn't for the likes of me,
They too would be looking for work.
These were its positive symptoms.

Its negative symptoms were extreme lethargy,
Laying in bed, sitting at home,
staring at the wallpaper.
Guilt, shame, depression,
and worrying about money.

He said, A lot of his patients had been complaining of the
same symptoms.
He took a prescription pad, saying,
"What do you want?"
"A decent job," I replied.
He smiled wryly,
And wrote me out a prescription for valium,
Saying, "Take one of these when it gets too bad,
"But not too many."
He's a good doctor.
He reached for the certificate pad;
"How long do you want?"
"Until the recession's over," I replied.
"Come and see me in a month," he said,
Handing me the note saying,
depression - a month off.
"Stop looking for work for a while,
"Don't even think about it.
"Do something worthwhile,
get meaning back in your life.
"Have a bit of fun, try to enjoy yourself.
"Take up a hobby. Try to get away.
"Anything but look for work."
I took his advice.
He's a good doctor.

MY ELECTRONIC LOVER

I'd like a computer woman,
An electronic lover,
An Android for a girl-friend,
Then I'd need no other.

She'd be built of the softest soft ware,
Touch sensitive technology,
She'd be ultra user friendly,
And programmed just for me.

She'd be tall and slim,
With golden red hair,
And curves in all the right places,
She'd have extra long legs,
Large bumps up top,
And a wardrobe full of faces.

I'd programme her my very own self,
The way that I'd want her to be,
With added bits by adventurous friends,
For unpredictability.

She'd be my dream,
My very own dream,
With her I'd want no other,
I'd throw away my little black book,
My electronic lover.

She'd never get a headache,
At night she'd never tire,
And if perchance she starts to nag,
I'd just twig a little wire.

The volume control would be near,
When we begin to talk,
She'd wash and dry the dishes,
And e'en take the dog for a walk.

She'd always be that magic age,
Her beauty will never fade,
She'd pour my drinks, light my fags,
And be my serving maid.

She'll never have women's problems,
We'll need no contraception.
And so I came up with this great idea,
The immaculate conception.

She'd be my dream,
My very own dream,
With her I'd want no other,
I'd throw away my little black book,
My electronic lover.

She'd always leave the toilet seat,
In the position I want it to be,
And she would quietly disappear,
When my best friends come to tea.

She'd let me watch the football,
And drink Newcastle Brown,
She'd always be a-singing,
And never wear a frown.

And if I get a headache,
And my mind goes all a-fug
Or if I want to be alone,
I'd simply pull the plug.

She'd be my dream,
My very own dream,
With her I'd want no other,
I'd throw away my little black book,
My electronic lover.

POETIC MOON BEAM

Summer love goddess
  of delicate rose petal proportions,
Lazy vision of delirious worship,
And sun shadowed forest
  of chanting diamonds,
Whisper sweet time in my sleep.

THE FIVE SENSES

I have seen mist rising from Scottish moorland,
I have seen Mount Vesuvious erupting,
I have seen stars falling from the sky,
But I have not seen you, my love, for ages.

I have heard the sound of silence booming in Leicester Square,
I have heard the sound of a curlew at full moon,
I have heard Angels speaking to me in hushed whispers,
But I have not heard you, my love, for ages.

I have touched Seventh Heaven,
I have touched rainbows in the night,
I have touched the top of a giant redwood tree,
But I have not touched you, my love, for ages.

I have smelt the sweet smell of success,
I have smelt rain falling through Amazonian Forests,
I have smelt rose petals in the snow,
But I have not smelt you, my love, for ages.

I have tasted honey dripping from the moon,
I have tasted the bitter sweet of life,
I have tasted strawberries and cream from Venus,
But I have not tasted you, my love, for ages.
.

JEAN CARDY

HUSBANDS
AETIOLOGY
QUEUING OUTSIDE THE UFFIZI
PAVLOVA'S COSTUMES
  (IN THE MUSEUM OF LONDON)

HUSBANDS

Husbands are precious.
They mend fuses,
Kill spiders,
Pay bills - some of them –
And are warm - or hot –
In bed.
Husbands are speech-friends,
So take care of them.
Life's cold without them.

Husbands are elusive.
They whore after golf,
Computer games,
Younger women.
But don't let go lightly.
Life's cold else.

Husbands are fragile.
They die sooner.
OAP coaches are full
Of fat jolly widows
And one gaunt, life-weary husband,
So take care of them.
Husbands are precious.
Life's cold without them.

AETIOLOGY

Today I learned a new word –
Aetiology means the projection of modern ideas
Into the past.
Your mind, which leapt to meet
Each new thing you encountered,
Is now stranded in the past,
Your feet trapped in concrete.
As I am carried away from you,
Your figure achingly tiny in the distance,
I project every new concept
Back to the touchstone of your judgement.
But the world changes.
Soon, if I live, I shall encounter
Things outside the parameters
Of your experience;
I must trudge on alone.

QUEUING OUTSIDE THE UFFIZI

We are today's pilgrims.
We travel much,
Suffer a little
For Art's sake.
We do not flagellate,
Do not wear away stone steps,
Ascending on our knees,
But we suffer a little
To pay homage
At the shrines
Of our gods.
We queue for two hours
To enter the Uffizi,
Stand faint in the sun
To behold Abu Simbel.
We do not fast
But we snatch strange snacks
To accommodate opening hours.
Thus we venerate
Michelangelo, Masacchio
And the nameless sculptors
Of antiquity –
Good-enough gods.

PAVLOVA'S COSTUMES
(IN THE MUSEUM OF LONDON)

Pavlova wore these flounces.
These goose feathers
Fluttered in a swan's death,
One wing left loose
For the dancer's hand to simulate
That dying tremble.
The skirts grew shorter
As time passed,
Supported on American tarlatan,
With softer undulation
Than modern nylon.
Bakst designed this dress;
Madame Mayna created it
On this dressmaker's form.
Hips and waist were small
But bust nicely rounded –
No modern anorexic here.
Her feet were size 4 and narrow
All that leaping failed
To coarsen and broaden.

And she was Russian
So there is one costume,
Long, heavy with jewels,
Collared,
Topped with a crescent headdress,
Tarnished gold in a bow
At the back,
Almost too heavy to dance in,
Worn only at those private functions
Where she helped to raise funds
For the wounded Russian soldiers
She cared about.

We came to breathe a legend,
Stayed to admire
The underpinning of that legend –
Sequins, sewn, not glued,
Ballet shoes, herring-boned to control
The bulge of a foot *en pointe*,
Giselle's wings, sprayed
To evoke mystery,
Steel bands
To be hidden under hair
To support shimmering
Fairytale headdresses,
Giant hooks
To keep trim bodices taut.

MARGARET PAZDZIERSKI

DEATH BY POETRY
HOW TO BE A MODERN POET
SHRAPNEL
RELUCTANT RIDER

DEATH BY POETRY

She died of terminal poetry
so the doctors said.
She'd suffered from it years,
but no one ever knew
until it started gushing from her ears -
her mouth - her every orifice.
Complex metaphors and epic similes
had blocked her vital organs.
Her sight had failed
and she could only see
through lenses tinged with purple prose,
and of her friends and neighbour
there were those
who privately believed she'd had a stroke,
though not - it must be said -
a stroke of genius.

HOW TO BE A MODERN POET
IN TEN EASY STAGES

One - Choose your topic.
    Any subject is permissible -
    ashtrays, chewing gum -
    as long as you keep emotion out of it.

Two - Write it down roughly on paper.
    It won't look anything like a poem at this stage,
    (or any stage come to that) but don't worry.

Three -Whatever you do, don't let it rhyme.
    unless you *cheat* and *sneak* in some *assonance*
    hoping no one notices the *difference*.

Four - Give it a
    strange rhythm with unexpected line
    breaks and no punctuation so that it's
    almost impossible to read aloud or read at all.

Five - Sprinkle it liberally with four letter words
    to show you're in touch with the real effing world.

Six - Hone it and hone it,
      (this can't be stressed enough)
      by cutting out all words but the most essential.
      The fewer the words that remain, the better
      for what you leave out is more important
      than what you leave in.

Seven- Type out your poem on your computer –
      and here you must be canny –
      never letting your computer see you blink,
      or, given half a chance,
      it will lose your poem completely
      or alter it beyond all recognition
      when you're not looking.

Eight - And this is the important bit –
      you must now put it away
      for several weeks
      till you've forgotten where you hid it
      in order to gain some objectivity.

Nine - And now the moment of truth –
      Take it out again (if you can find it),
      read through it objectively and exclaim
      'What a load of garbage!'

Ten - The final stage -
      Screw, it up and throw it in the bin,
      vowing never to do it again -
      until the next time.

SHRAPNEL

Today I finally put you away –
it was time –
but I had to wait till the pangs of loss
had grown dull-edged,
till the vest of lead I had worn inside for so long
had corroded,
had broken into fragments and dissolved
like icicles pressed against warm flesh,
slowly,
painfully,
until just one flint-hard fragment remained –   *remains.*
So today I was able to put you away –
the photos,
the letters,
the books inscribed 'with affection' –
everything I had left of you,
locked away in a box
in the attic,
so final, like a burial ⁄

except that one day,
when, as an old woman
I am sorting through my store of memories
with arthritic fingers,
I shall dig you up again
and examine your mortal remains
fondly, with a smile,
marvelling at such foolishness ⁄

though the fragment
will still give me a twinge now and then,
in cold damp weather perhaps,
or when dusk falls on a soft summer evening.

RELUCTANT RIDER

Time has kicked over the traces
and is running wild,
with me, a reluctant rider
clinging to his neck.
And he has no harness
for me to rein him in
and I'm riding bareback.
And he's galloping too fast
for me to leap off –
and there's an ill wind blowing.

And my hands are growing numb
from clinging to his neck
and my knees are stiff
from gripping his flanks,
and I can't see where I'm going
for his mane is lashing my face
and tears are stinging my eyes,
but he just gnashes his teeth
and snorts at my distress –
and there's a shrill wind blowing.

And he gallops faster, faster,
and l know he'll never stop
until he finally throws me off,
and though l cling on now,
screaming like a madwoman,
in the end the throwing off
will come as a relief,
for icicles are forming
in my head and in my heart –
and there's a chill wind blowing.

BETTY HILL

COMMUNICATION
SPRING CHORUS
A WEIGHTY PROBLEM
HUMAN KITTENS
PEBBLES ON THE SHORE

COMMUNICATION

He's got hisself a mobile phone.
and stuck it in his ear.
He'll need an operation.
To get it out of there.

"Hi there." He says with flourish
"I'm speaking from the train.
I want to talk to PJ
About Australian grain?"

He calls himself CT.
And makes sure we all hear.
Just how important he is.
With the phone in his ear.

I expect he'll find out
That PJ had to go.
They couldn't afford him.
His phone calls, you know!

They said it was not
The cost of the call.
The price of the mobile
Was nothing at all.

But time that was wasted.
By people at base.
Taking meaningless calls.
Was really the case.

So PJ was redundant.
He wasn't alone.
CT will soon follow
Along with his phone!

SPRING CHORUS

Come sit with me and we will sing
A song of joy because it's Spring
The birds are nesting in the trees
Blossoms float down on the breeze
A petal carpet coats the lawn
A lark soars high above new corn
Come my love and sing our lays
Of shorter nights and longer days
Your eyes are bright as twinkling stars
My love is deep, there are no bars
I promise to be always true
Can I say the same of you?
The season makes the heart beat fast
But is our love ordained to last?
Come sit by me upon the wall
And wake the neighbours with our caterwaul.

A WEIGHTY PROBLEM

It can't be right, I'm not that fat
These scales are wrong, I bet.
I'll twiddle the knob and try again.
Just let me get it set!

It's still the same as yesterday,
I hardly ate a thing.
And all that walking, swimming too ...
I'll just take off my ring.

My glasses too, they weigh a bit,
Now I can't see the dial.
I'll put them back, take out my teeth,
And breathe in for a while.

I might as well give up the diet,
The tasteless veggie food,
I try and try and still stay fat
It's never any good.

It isn't fair that I'm so fat,
No-one could call me greedy.
Others eat voraciously
And look so thin and weedy.

HUMAN KITTENS

They really are annoying,
And make such dreadful noise
I wish they'd go away and play,
With other girls and boys.

Just when I've washed my face and paws
And settled for a nap
They grab me round the middle
And sit me on their lap.

They tie a ribbon round my neck
Sometimes they even try
To dress me in a silly frock.
It really makes me cry.

No matter how I squawk and growl
They carry on regardless
And dance with me around the room
Until I'm nearly senseless.

If they were mine, I tell you now.
I'd know just what to do.
I'd wallop them, and wash them well.
And sell them to a zoo.

PEBBLES ON THE SHORE

Even the biggest pebble on the sand
Which does not shift in the ferocious tide
Shines for just a moment
As the torrent washes over
Before our eyes are dazzled the lustre fades
It becomes once more dull stone.
Mightier than others, for a time
Until eroded to grains of sand.

Man craves eternity, to shine above
Those around him. In the end his power crumbles.
The only control he keeps is of himself
Familiar structures are dashed away.
Different values shape the world.
Status has no place within the new edifice.
The highest must eventually retreat to join the crowd
Clamouring to support new masters.

ISHI FUDÉ

BARKING MAD
SUBWAY STRAP HANGIN'
STEAMING STREETS
THE LISTENING WALL
OFF YA TROLLEY
CADFLY
TIGER TIGER

BARKING MAD

"You've talked me into it!"
The man said.

I hadn't said a word.

"The price is right you know it."
The man said.

I didn't believe what I heard.

"Tell you what I'll do, Sir."
The man said.

I was about to walk away.

"A special price just for you, Sir."
The man said.

So I decided to stay.

"Not a Tenner or Fiver!"
The man said.

Looking furtive around.

"It's the bargain of a life, Sir!"
The man said.

So I bought 2 for a pound.

> Now I'm not stupid,
> or nothing like that,
> but walking away with
> 2 cigarette lighters
> when I don't even smoke,
> is making me feel such a Charlie,
> a real proper prat!

SUBWAY STRAP HANGIN'

Hanging onto a strap, the world is submerged
and flashes by in bits between the black.
Swaying like a hypnotized snake, inside a
hypnotized snake, the blink of an eye catches
glimpses of one of those 'bits' ....N SQU...
passing by. Too fast to read. Too tired to care.
Back into the dark walled cocoon, a silent,
rumbling womb, swallowing - disgorging -
swallowing - us whole.

Thoughts as blurred as the vista, wonder
is there any sense in the advertising pictures
and graffiti jostling for space before each
 weary blank and bleary, expressionless face.

A forest of arms, all dutifully latched onto a strap
bear ticking fruit. On each a ripe wrist watch.
Time becomes evident, imposing itself,
as these forest fruits argue - none agreeing
the minutes, though consensus is reached
as to the hour.

As time and train move ever on, one by one
the straps release their grip, and the belly
of the snake empties.

Instinct evolved over an eon of journeys,
causes a pre-emptive flicker of consciousness
.....R STR... is a popular stop.
Nearly all the snake fodder clambers off.
Only one remains.
My stop is next.

STEAMING STREETS OF BROADWAY

Steam in the streets, like some ancient mythic beast,
deep underground that wakes breathing steam.

Deep underground, hot is hot. That means steam.
Steam on the sidewalks.
Steam in the coffee cups,
a caffeine kick to start the city up.

Up before the sun.
Up before the cars.
Up before the honking horns, the sirens,
the anger and angst of the beast awake.

Awake is later. Later than the steam.
After the dark.
After the steam.

Awake is when the sun burns away the steam.
Awake is when the sun sets on frying sidewalks.
Hot sidewalks –
        hot with heels,
        hot with desire,
        hot with neon.

After the neon the beast sleeps –
                for those few moments
when night breaks into light and
steam rises from the streets.

THE LISTENING WALL

The wall has long since gone,
yet somewhere memories linger on,
of children's marks in children's chalk,
on that listening wall to children's talk.
All knocked down so as to make way,
for a concrete place for cars to play.

A lone oak tree in a Park.
Two hearts carved deep into its bark.
Sealing a teenage lovers vow.
Meant truly then, but broken now.

The tree still stands,
but in strange surrounds.
Alone, just as it was before,
only now outside a superstore.

Where once grass grew by and by,
here shoppers rush through buy and buy.
So hungry for so much to eat,
that trees and grass must all retreat.

Amid the noise of busy lives,
the listening wall is silent.

OFF YA TROLLEY

The young checkout girl is shopping
                              while she works.
She likes the busy late shift best.
For one thing the continuous stream of packets
and tins tumbling along the rubber belt
keeps her well manicured hands busy.

The hands that busily ring the till have rings
                              on every finger -
except third finger left hand. That gap in her
golden adornment is what <u>she</u> is shopping for,
each night she works the late shift,
at the supermarket store.

Every trolley gets the eye, to see if it belongs
to some handsome guy, who will whisk her away
in his car outside. A Porsche would be nice.

As the last basket at the end of another fruitless
shift drops out of sight, she sighs,
"I must be off my trolley!"

CADFLY

'Dangerous, Dangerous'
the cadfly groans -

as Goffins convert their currency of greed.
No folly can ever surpass,
a farmer selling his stock of seed.
So grows the grass, long and reaching.

Wait ye by the marram flow,
where wind does wave the long tall grass,
to point the way for us to go,
far out to sea in a little boat,
with no sail to return us home.

Wait ye there when the moon is round,
and full as apples on an orchard bough.
Be silent there don't make a sound,
'till sunrise starts the cock to crow.

As night shrinks back its star clad cape,
let us gaze dawn's embrace, then run
hand in hand 'cross dunes of sand,
to the waters edge.
Together there, to seal our fate.

TIGER TIGER

Tiger - Leap
Tiger - Dart
Tiger - Pad your way through jungle dark.

Tiger - Hunt
Tiger - Run
Tiger - Shot through the head by distant gun.

Tiger - Rug
Tiger - Bone
Tiger - Less, since you're dead and gone.

So who now frames thy fearful symmetry?

Western whores, adorned with strip'ed fur;
Eastern heathens, are eating magic bones;
And your jungle den is hacked aside -
To make way for those who revere you.

Our zoos may be your last reward,
As you pounce from advertising boards.
Man salutes such wondrous mask,
While poets pen thy epitaph.

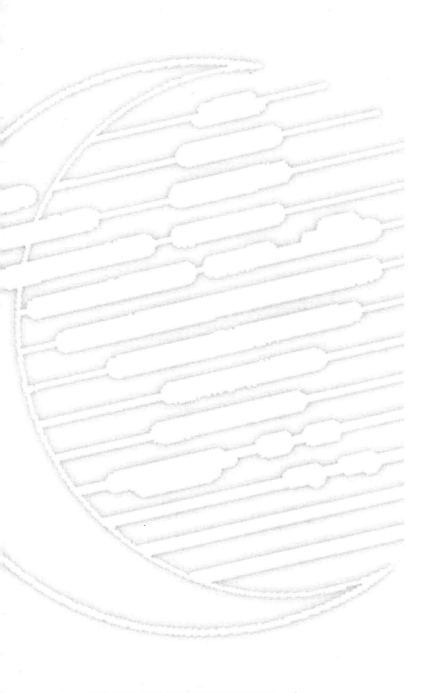

HUNGRY OWL PUBLICATIONS LTD, London
Website : www.hungryowlbooks.com